Irish Arts Center

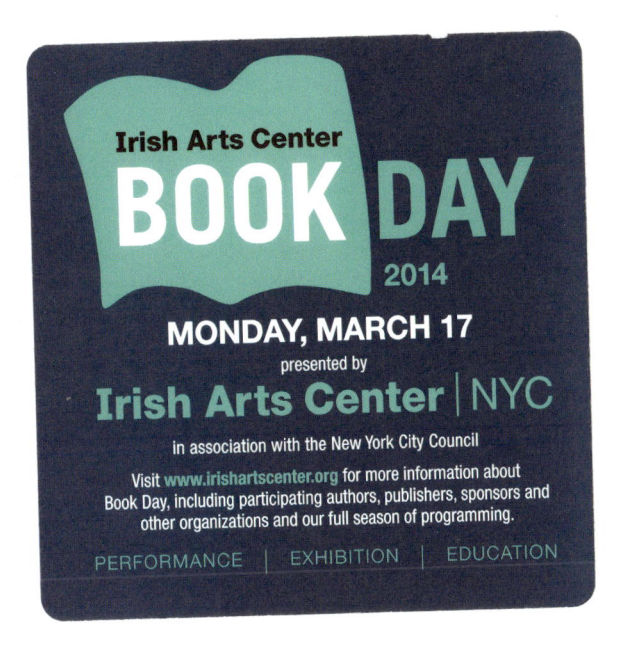

BOOK DAY

2014

MONDAY, MARCH 17

presented by

Irish Arts Center | NYC

in association with the New York City Council

Visit www.irishartscenter.org for more information about Book Day, including participating authors, publishers, sponsors and other organizations and our full season of programming.

PERFORMANCE | EXHIBITION | EDUCATION

WEXFORD AND ARCADY

James Liddy

WEXFORD AND ARCADY

ARLEN
HOUSE

© James Liddy, 2009

The moral rights of the author have been asserted.

Published in 2009 by
ARLEN HOUSE
an imprint of Arlen Publications Ltd
PO Box 222
Galway
Phone/Fax: 353 86 8207617
Email: arlenhouse@gmail.com

Distributed in North America by
SYRACUSE UNIVERSITY PRESS
621 Skytop Road, Suite 110
Syracuse, NY 13244–5290
Phone: 315–443–5534/Fax: 315–443–5545
Email: supress@syr.edu

ISBN 978–1–903631–96–6,
(a signed and numbered limited edition is also available)

Typesetting | Arlen House
Printing | Betaprint

Contents

Arcady
- 15 In The Red Bank Restaurant
- 16 Rome
- 18 Un Rechaud
- 20 I Visit the Upper Chamber and Flee
- 21 Cocktail on the Trays
- 26 Molten
- 27 To the Counts Von Stauffenberg
- 28 The Nation
- 30 Ex Sean O Tuama
- 31 Snippets of Altar Ballads
- 33 Happy Easter
- 34 Being a Jacobite
- 36 I have driven through the dark night of my soul
- 37 Lament for the Queen of James II
- 38 Dans le restaurant
- 39 O Bella Roma
- 44 Listening to the Radio in the 1940s
- 46 Bloomsday Souvenir

Wexford
- 49 Two Postcards
- 50 Wexford Notaí
- 51 Inoffensively in Wexford
- 53 Stevie's Wild Ashes
- 55 All Around My Hat I Wear Peace Coloured Ribbons O
- 58 Christmas Eve
- 59 Christmas Eve 1950
- 60 Mother Goes Home
- 62 Tom Walsh, K.M.
- 64 Omos do Funge
- 65 Enda Keane, O.F.M.

67 May, Queen of Inch
68 That House Again
70 Dead Tennis Court
72 I Sing of the English
74 Fire Phoenix Pyre
75 Life of the Fianna
76 Jacobins
77 Evensong in Wexford Town
78 At Your Holy Mouth

80 About the Author

Acknowledgements

Acknowledgements are made to the following journals: *Blue Canary, Legal Studies Forum, Meeting Eyes Bindery, Poetry Ireland Review, The SHOp.*

For Clare on the day
when Compton MacKenzie
was in her house.

The Churches of Arcady are no longer
full, love and loneliness are on the streets.

Arcady

In The Red Bank Restaurant

Sam Sam the Ginger Man
I follow you to the zenith
Guy Fawkes man in bonfire

Just by accident saw you on
Trinity cobble stones behind
the beadles stonestaring

In D'Olier Street a trifle silly
last big Protestant shadow
on our underpass underbelly

Swift and his serving man
through the Liffey monsoon
will never keep up with Sam

look us rich kids sort of fey
no serving man at luncheon
but in a decent restaurant

Sam take a Guinness soon
in the bright oyster afternoon
strip naked in the month of May

1959

Rome

Let me speak of myself before I talk
about Miss Bowen. I was in the city
between her two visits, in 1950.
Sun trucks sun roofs glittered for me
railway workers clenched their iron fists.

But yes I would have liked the pre-war
bedded blue irises before much
of the Palatine was excavated,
though Rome is anti-romantic to
Romans we are citizens of that city.

Amid palaces and terraced gardens
we were Cromwellians in awe
of mystery: Miss Bowen with her
northern mansion, me with blood of
border guards to shut the Irish in Clare.

Miss Bowen the whig who wants
a radical Cromwell/Garibaldi in
the Alban hills, she has *The Brook Kerith*
in her blood dissecting St. Paul's arrest
from the angle of citizenship.

I myself put on Cromwellian war paint,
intermarriage transforms it
to Catholic Church hue, Domus Aurea:
I too eyed a scarlet spiked gladioli tree
in front of Pius XII, holy his glasshouse.

I read Miss Bowen, my cousin Kate
O'Brien I adore with family eclat,
let Miss Bowen and I pray at carnival
may Venus glance towards our paint
and can we borrow Cupid's arrows?

UN RECHAUD
for Matt Glynn

I saw F.J. McCormack
I heard Ruth Draper doing her maid's Co. Kerry
Father liked 'The Shadow of the Glen' he wanted to be
    a tramp
Yeats's plays my favourites tacked on at the end for a
    quarter of the house
I preferred MacLiammoir in 'The Old Lady Says No' in
    the
Gate to his 'The Importance of Being Oscar' in the
    Gaiety
Siobhan McKenna St. Joan of all St. Joans
    MacLiammoir
as evil Warwick Edwards as Cauchon big ruby ring on
    finger
Jackie McGowran crouching back of stage terrified
    Dauphin
Clapping Kavanagh at 'Tarry Flynn' curtain 'It's a
    failure'
Sam stole Yeats's and Synge's beggar rags made them
    more radiant
at the Pike second English production of 'Waiting for
    Godot'

And years afterwards
sat in Milwaukee in the bar for Chris O'Neill's Beckett
    Behan
and 'The Importance of being Oscar' then Chris started
    on Frank
Dermody strutting like a rabbit in the after hours rabbit
    hole
the Manhattan or Behan a poseur nude star at the 40
    foot

The parade of pints downed like
galleons on the rocks of Clare
let's bend down for Chris's bags
enroute to Tomas and Nora's car
in the Black Shamrock's parking lot

If there was a house next door
a drink would be poured through
the hall door of the night 'Not one
for the ditch but one before the dawn'
come Actor bow blow a Guinness
or whiskey kiss from those lips
hold your friend Liam Miller's hand
ghosts in antic boards' azure

I Visit the Upper Chamber and Flee

My uncle-in-law the Clerk of the Senate
invited me there on a day in 1950,

a few pinkcheeked cherubs
round Lord Longford, Michael Yeats

the State's sister held together by
Celtic broaches safety pins (O unlit

fuse) Senator Miss Margaret Pearse,
she a young-men-sender-out-to-die:

This young man set out for necking in
the woods of another country which is

maybe not Arcady – know the place by a
feast of the immaculate movement on hips.

Cocktail on the Trays

Saturday Lederhosen band
arms around each other closely:
I didn't feel too bad, I felt
more a Black than a Jew.

Reproach of Jesus Over Dublin
I fed you alcoholic drinks
in the colonial desert
and you trekked from
churches into condos.

St. Patrick's Day, 2007
I fled to a Schlitz parlour with a woman who has lived
in San Francisco for 40 years who told me her father
used to work in the giant car factory opposite. Looking
into the bar she said, 'There used to be a popcorn
machine in that corner'. Her mother had been a nurse in
the factory, 400 men and a woman, and her father won
her by getting on his knees to recite a Yeats poem. I
said, 'Brown penny, brown penny'. She replied, 'How
did you know that?'

Concertina Bar: I liked
the accordion lark/nightingale
Vincy's in Coolgreany
I saw the ark in my mind
danced before it in my mind,
but this polka dance place
stinks of WWII the Luftwaffe
over Coolgreany turn east to
bomb the shit out of Cardiff
Forgive them, though
they caressed their bombs ...

Reproach of Jesus Over The Coasts
I am a Jew, I lead you in a pillar
of cloud over Croagh Patrick
I gave you tea and water from
the holy well, you gave me a
pogrom, you excluded me
in the 1930s from your shores.

In the parlour the woman had another story. When in the 1880s a fire devastated the Third Ward all the Irish Catholic houses burned down. The one Protestant house was left standing. Her great grandfather the immigrant standing in the water watched. 'The Devil protected that house', I said. 'How did you know he said that?, she asked.

'The Irish folk mind'.
The barley-shaking wind
doesn't shake mine except for
The Irish Free State 1922-32,
lawyers farmers who shouldered
in absurd actual gravitas
for a gorgeous decade the State.
Apres cela l'abime.[1]

Reproach of Jesus over Doughmore
Donn na Duimche, you divided
the place with me, you the fairy
palace inside sandhills,
me the church up the road:
why did you let Americans
Japanese Dublin tourists
bulldoze your tall wild hills
and empty my Sunday sanctuary
to make golf courses?

In the parlour I was with the women and two beautiful
youths, a Kavanagh seducee and a Pogues bewitched, a
working Pabst can team. The woman made a mistake,
she said, 'Why don't you go to San Francisco and be
lovers?' Disgust on cherub faces

Reproach of Jesus over Galway
I hid with you in the bog
in the secret Catholic gentry's attics
I got your children
to the schoolmaster,
you turned me out on the street
as if you were dealing with
a Jewish peddler
a patent medicine quack.

I am the king of the great Clock Tower
and I am the king of Shillelagh woods
I am the king of the Banner county
my name is de Clare and I build castles.[2]
Let's all go drinking at the well
where beauty is handcuffed haunted
let's all go this very moment to watch
if beauty will be released today.
Let's all hurry to the well because
the English soldiers are going to depart
there is foreboding they are handsome
their gold will not linger in the street.
Girls will be widowed boys unattended
potency a small item in the The Cause.
The kings like Henry will bulldoze
the Church and proclaim it soiled[3]
the Kings will make a Parliament
declare the priests lay over-white
hands on the knees of the princes.
Beauty a prisoner in a cold well.

Okay we were not born from the Treaty of Versailles, it came out of Gen. Collins's revolver. But A.E's bust waits in Merrion Sq. leaves to be unveiled. Garret the Silken the Astute came out of the door of Government Buildings, we watched him walk across to the park. He was accompanied by an aide. Reminiscence about the honoured one known on his father's knee at tea. On sun-trumpeted grass the beauty of the Anglo-Irish avatars of the passion for the state. The brother of Flann O'Brien ranged beside us. We dreamt dream in Georgian sunlight decorating ourselves in an ethereal garden.[4]

Reproach of Jesus over the Phoenix Park
I hovered kitelike over the grass
I lay on the grass I squinted at the
Papal Nunciature I saw dogs' heads,
McCormack's voice like kindling
expostulation of the Jewish king,
I died again my thorns dipped
on the deer the polo grounds.

Brian Arkins phones,
'The election seems close,
it depends on the small parties,
the Greens will be in Government'.
I ask, 'Wasn't Ireland always green'.

Yes but darker green my Maying
costume, all around my hat I wear
black for the useless holocausts.

Notai
[1] All from Gen. Collins's
down-well eyes from
his edgy certain mouth

from his revolvers both gold
and silver
swayed in many hands.

2. Ahearn is not crowned
King of Ireland
at Tara ... which he sold.

3. The anti-pedophile candidate
got his vote in North Wexford
from the liberals about Tara Hill.

4. King Oedipus
In the end
like her
liked only
Fine Gael
Roman Church.

Molten

An uncle philandered in Berlin and Hamburg in the 30s
parks of summer Nordics
warm combed skin on beaches
my uncle got one last beautiful girl
Linden trees Kaiser-friendly
my uncle spoke of a rose garden at the
fringe of a Potsdam lake
splash of eels and mermaids
I go to the parade in lake-cool then warming
    Milwaukee
boys and girls in Berlin/Hollywood cream facade
territory of beautiful pagans
You have to replay courtship
of how to make a difference for those
lovely without relief
plucking these cinders out of the fire
(if you're famous for monologue you end in duet)
in a vale of ambivalence and inclination
steins of beer in Lake Michigan shining moon
I toast posh Weimars and honeyed Goethes
to sweeten these brows in the universe
planning them in rosebuds and water
Delicate inverted task
to refurbish the sheet music
of an uncle's recharging heat

To the Counts Von Stauffenberg

The poet loved three beautiful boys
and in the courtyards of the Bendlerstrasse
Hitler the thief forced to admit
the officer corps had broken their oaths to him.

Do not underestimate the effect of
a queer poet on heterosexual young men
one half of romanticism
is contained in that sentence,
have women, marry—this may
happen—but you have to find a man
a Monsieur Verlaine a Herr George,
a task is contained in that sentence
that of avoiding the domestic.
Stefen George fell in love with the sons
of the chamberlain of Wurttemburg,
like a Venus out of a shell
with Berthold, as if he were Parsifal
with Claus, as if he were the owl
of Minerva with Alexander.
The writing of a poem can elope
into a bomb in a briefcase
that can shake the dead gods out
of the dead Black Forest.
To kill a thief of millions of men
bishop-sanctioned act of elegance.

A young man liberated
can come up to you with that
secret Germany in his eyes
that secret yearning or taste, that
clandestine pact, even in Milwaukee.

The Nation

Forked paths of gold
acrobatic aesthetics
folk lighthouses on the lakes—
we thought for a moment they
do what we are doing
but they are day star people
gold cart people,
their settlements paid for
by Cupid's high arm,
night mothers, day son
at a wake as swans in a film.

Songs that drink themselves
to songs like desserts.
We removed ourselves
from wall cloths of gold
was it silver where two
tongues did tavern-bow,
where we were bothered
by doubts on supernatural
agencies—the Yeatses
lured us back luted us back.
They wore our pearls on stage
the fair turned into fairyland,
fairy lore to love creatures
in animal and spirits.

So in the real country now
fairy boys talk only to the girls,
given ancient fates so late.
& for Anne Yeats,
she was a wake gilded by swans
a camera that took golden snaps
a white flower in a hot house

a cup of holy well water more
than an interpretive center.

Ex Sean O Tuama

Straight poet on the beach
in a straight country Greece,
sobbed on three gone, File,
Ceoltoir, an Maistir-Saoi,

three muses with man faces
'tortured' queer poet, music
goboy and whiskey bottle,
not so 'tortured' dandy.

This Gael lifts himself
up for a solo dance on
the Apollo tourist sand
throws out his legs –

wants to melt in the sun
blurred moment –
check him out boys
from hedges far away.

Snippets of Altar Ballads

You fell in love with cranks
you fell in love with the city
you fell for the cranky in the city
most you remember you served
as an altar boy in the city
you an offering on the altar

You spied out the city
that was God's city when
you were an altar boy and
the priest wasn't looking
you noticed around you
outrageous acts of clemency

Prayers said nothing is simple
but this may be more simple
the hymns egged you on
to be God or just a priest
when you lifted the vestment
you got a cracked sense of God

The faithful at the altar vowed
a demonstration started in the
street of your head against the
sweet who can be brokered
to pews that exclude cranks
stay single in a sweet sweat

A better decked out altar
you held hands right in
the face of Clemency that is
reflected in the altar cloth
our hands hold a thousand
hours' sweetheart reflections

Til the city collects saints
til we enter our priesthoods
til simplicity becomes clemency
til the altar flowers rumble
til the candle smoke hymns
til our hands hold the sun's reflection

Happy Easter

Why do we call last Friday good, because on this day there was a supper party, first of a few.

For liturgical reasons I'm thinking of Austin Clarke, apostate, I hardly ever think of him. I remember in his autobiography he talks of doing the seven churches on Maundy Thursday around Dublin, where there were flowers though it was the sad season, I suppose. Indulgences? I did them with my aunt Gertie from Donnybrook to Rathgar, I think Austin and I had several churches in common specially Tranquilla Convent upper Rathmines Road (polished floor of the Carmelites).

A little volume for my birthday, does my sex life need this kind of advertisement? Dear Jesus Christ, you alone look beautiful you alone should have wild parties. Will friends write little ditties for me?

Re Celtic/Anglo-Irish Eden/Arcadia that was childhood with Clare Maggie and Josie in the house bitter very sweet society, after it you had to find a common dancing area between church and body.

I remember being in a bar with Austin after the Living Art Exhibition opening and saying to him and Nora, 'With the changes in the Council you will be trekking back?' Austin was old, 'I will consider that much later'. Donagh MacDonagh and Nuala were sitting with us smoking cigarettes, I thought of the Fourth Eclogue, *desinet ac toto surget gens aurea mundo/casta fave Lucina ...'* I imagined Austin again, 'No'.

Me though – never able to hang up the party's shoes.

BEING A JACOBITE
(In Charleston)

On Wentworth Street kings float over the water
Stuart kings who flower in from the sea
by the naval base by heaven and hell
shapes and bricks of a noble sense,
artillery like a giant's fist
rice and cotton in the lowlands
silver and gold like dune pebbles
arched walkways to church doors,
in the cemetery of the Huguenot church
berries on the holly trees (round leaves
not the pointed ones at Dingle)
Spanish moss weeping into fountains,
from the fountains I have cried for what:
I've floated from the Song of Songs
my mind has gone upstairs,
this is not the French Quarter
its licentious soldiery drunk in bed
so I cockcade down Wentworth St
a Munster aisling for the princes
in the ink in my pen in my pocket.
The columned Lutheran church
effervesces in white over its memorial stones
I see a matchstick old orange house
room only for an army of mice to march
the stairs must have flown from Titania's palace
fairies in Kerry in a gale wind to here
to enact a wonderful masque in January,
large yellow butterfly surfaces
from the shrubbery green-tinged wings
milling like oars above water
next a medium mansion with a portico
a flight of white cream steps to the side
a plate 'The Convent of St. Catherine',

a frail black nun in old habit walks
rosary-like beside the butterfly conjunction:
the soul and a holy lady from the ancient past.
Richard has walked off to the markets
thinking of crab cakes and red beans and rice
but I rest in the glade of my heart
in the cold heaven thickets of a royal city
and find my day in sun butterfly and nun
find my queen Catherine of Braganza.

I have driven through the dark night of my soul
with my wine lips hovering in the glass
to toast the princes on St. Peter's pillar.
May the King across the water travel back
over the water, may he be trumpeted
to Whitehall in a four white horse carriage,
may his Polish Queen have comfort
the three kingdoms at his feet a basket of
puppies ... Tony Burgess's father dying
enjoined, 'I'll be with King James tonight
in heaven, never dine with Hanoverian swine'.
I have not taken the soup though in love
with the great grandsons of British soldiers.

LAMENT FOR THE QUEEN OF JAMES II

The stone laid over braid glitter
smooth forehead cheeks light
a vase of rose

fair body structure the berry
that shone inside it.

Glory a virtue a conceit
a term of rhetoric benignly
attached to your name Mary ...

Your death day thick thunder
old people yelling prayers

Princess with deep throat Death
winter-cold these wake drinks.

From the Irish of O' Neachtan

Dans le restaurant

Liddy: 'You were born the same week as The Pope?'
Archbishop Weakland: 'He's nine days younger;
you're old when you're older than The Pope'.

Liddy: 'These almost Popes almost Bishops!'
Archbishop Weakland: 'I remember an almost
Pope Siri of Genoa on a Roman beach in full
black bathing costume paddling in the water'.

Archbishop Weakland: 'If God exists ...
Liddy: 'When he exists ...'
Weakand & Liddy: 'We want another Council'.

O Bella Roma

I

Poems, scraps of writing, whispers even, of what I have brought to some young men I fall in love with, with glances and then with words that I have tried from voices of poets I eared and eyed in my youth then the words that tuned together in my mind from what Jesus and Socrates said to their young men and they kissed them in some way, I'm sure but I haven't always kissed as in some cases not appropriate but I bent to the lips most times specially earlier, it's all salutation: Bless what was at first your shivery or panic selves in presence of god or gods with libation before and during deepset lovespake handshake, I address you in what will ever be the sweet homes of your bodies, gave you what maybe you didn't appreciate initially hormone cadence that through its shiny aesthetics sweats out drips out poetry, art.

Not pillows in trains nor diamond lights transported in helicopters as I carried a suitcase of sentiments via Ryan Air to the Eternal City, I spread the paragraphs of my feelings Greek love between men and young men under the white hem and red slippers of Holiness that knows these ancient mixtures of Attic and Semitic piping poet gazed at shepherd and turned devout figures in a landscape, Holiness tread serenely with the attitude of a saint or with the nice patriarch's politeness on this ornately disguised truthfulness this canon of transcendence formulating in desire swoop gently to release these attachments through the columns sparkle of fountains, encase them with other precious items in the jewelry box of a formidable beautiful German and Latin.

II

Celtic harp
malingering
woody patois.

Monumental
brunch of bricks
street valley

green shutters
flowers illuminate trumpet

centuries of sweet incense
hunger of women
not to surrender

Sisters of St. Augustine
in crumbling 4th century
bricks blow out
candles at Vespers.

Parenting drifts
the flowers.

Divan
stirring

accompanied by powerful
dreams of toes
and ankles.

Coliseum nearby
but the perfume
is from shop counters:

Miss Reeves
Miss Bowen
each one ration
of Oliver Cromwell.

City of staring clerks

Roman streets
are also sedatives.

Miss Reeves children

Miss Bowen volumes

terror at childbearing

terror of sentences' beginning.

Women came into their own
in Rome a dream
of siestas.

The musk scent is
my mother.

   III

Domus Aurea

He was that kind of bastard
20th century style
I'm a bastard of a different dance style
I supped stepped out
into the revealing glare of love mirror
with America's sweethearts
middle to moderate punks
but Nero's was the ultimate hooley
or weekend massive buttocks of bricks
deep recessing into windows doors
wild flowers little dances in the grass outside
plumbago oleander in two hues
at a distance from the walls.
What is a party if it hasn't intervals
for tweaking grasses and glasses
breaks for clear flat thoughts?
Party skills are passed on.
Walking in the park I was taken
with an inordinate whim for champagne.

   IV

From Tuborg in the restaurant
to folklore flowers around Nero's house
plumbago and oleander, the last

a rich poison. Ignoring the lions
the robed cardinals why didn't
some Christians feed doses to
John Paul II in a dark dungeon
under this park until he withered?

    V

At the Coliseum

Where are you from?
I'm from San Diego.
I'm from Lexington.
We're all English majors.
Gladiator cries
in the soft popular culture
centre of Rome.

Listening to the Radio in the 1940s

I heard two voices when I was young with dead nightingales making sonata sounds in them, with dark muttering from Elizabethan drama and the prayer of a Russian gambler after he left the casino with a girl and no gold, with choristers with high sexual makeup that hung low throwing flowers or petals in polyphonic registers, that then shot up out of the ocean to entangle in slivers of moonlight that was the soda water in the glass of radium. On reflection these voices seemed two versions of a holy ghost battered by two European wars, of cities that stopped dead in their tracks on a realisation the barbarians sat within hiring the previous police force, that civility might have begun and ended with the star cries of boys that brought Vergil his cups of wine. The lamplighters in the gardens of the west were smashing their lamps not by accident, I had to listen to the blessed recusant William Byrd for half an hour to reengage the dual sounds.

These voices were not those of knights in the yard below though their part origins came from the throats of elaborate blanketed horses nor from sighing of servants to whom commands floated down staircases a rollcall. My shining auditory crystals had lain among the jeweled crusts of gold monstrances, had lain deep in the dug ground when Reformation looters had plundered the deep beating heart of shrines, when the trustees of rationality had dispensed with the god bread and wine of the poor that kept them alive more than alive caps in the air when facing daily and weekly death. My tongues had stood under the tree when the Princess from Heaven with her sweet darling had hovered above in the dress of the last ultimate spring a routine so normal and unfathomable that people came every hour out of wine shops to join in hymning, the accents unfurling within them would slow the rotting cities from sinking would prop up towards the clouds the crashed buildings would start flower beds beneath the gaps showing in the roofs.

The cities' fall stalled because the holy shrines have opened their hands that are radios at night onto the street and to people in the threatened houses. Turn the knob. So I will pull back the shades of 1944 to reveal haloes that sparkled through loud or quiet speakers over the smoking massacres of the tyrants over the propaganda became more perilous than bombs and rockets, I attest to the mouths of those that served as icons of broadcast that peeled bells the all clear for humanity. Four eyes that remembered peace for saints and poets had kept records of how to petition for peace. I heard placarded in rhythm in resonance in a neutral house in Ireland from my father's dial the voice with doves walking or whispering in it of Pius XII's 'Sursum corda', or T.S. Eliot's Aeniad-tone spotting across river from Lambeth Palace the Luftwaffe who couldn't topple St. Paul's dome.

Bloomsday Souvenir

I was looking out the Bailey window I saw Georgio
Joyce and his wife (recognised them from newspapers)
peering in the windows. The look on his face: I think
that's them in there, them Joyceans sweating over
those pages, converts to Dublin streets, impressarios
about my family. If we go in there will be nothing to
say, we need a drink. I went out on the street to follow
the couple, they moved further down to just outside
the Duke Lounge, peering in another window, in
debate with each other. I caught his similar look: a
plainer crowd, businessmen working men,
not book worms, not US campus pint drinkers, not the
local Dedalus flavour of the day, not John Ryan, not
Michael Scott, not Ronnie Drew ...
could we go in, be Irish? They pushed the door to booze
and ice in hand, I peering through the glass at them.

Wexford

Two Postcards

This what the railway company did for whiskey.
The Rosslare train stopped on the right bank
of the River Slaney. Sir John Powers and family
left their carriage to walk down the few steps
to a small pier where a boatman was waiting
to row them over the river to Edermine House.

General Moran was modest about being a General.
'There are many Generals in the British Army'.
There was a pool near Auckavanagh hunting lodge.
The Redmonds invited Moran a young Unionist
to dip in it with them. The General said, 'John was
reticent but a gentleman. Willie was a charmer'.

WEXFORD NOTAÍ

The man said, 'The day held', on
the Main Street. 'Safe home
and don't go to the clubs',
the barman said.

Old port city with the wave
intensity of a swan in the Faythe,
the wicked swan is vicious but
the pints are as sweet as Viking
sugar; 19th century river port city.

Looking west: to carry perhaps the mind
of a writer out of the bogs; Master, shall
I find the chalice in marl or bog cotton?

A lifetime is an opportunity to converse
about oneself but some voice takes over.

He loved me from the beginning and still
loves me from somewhere I don't know;
or she loved me from the beginning and
still loves me somewhere I don't know.

The Wicked Swan's rest places were
marked cobs and swans; I felt faint like
Edmund Spenser, Eric entered a strange door.

INOFFENSIVELY IN WEXFORD

When I hear Mozart playing
on the radio in Mary Street
I think of my father being
present at his own opera festival
in the theatre around the corner
tenors and sopranos his crowd
librettos his truest wife.

At the priest's party
the P.P. asked me if I wanted
the Church of Ireland room
or the one with the singles.
I went to the first
the one with wives,
we talked about the gentry.
They thought I was one of them,
'We had your bishop
from Milwaukee, a Yorkshire man,
you've got to get oil quickly if you bore'.
I thought of the murmured vows
of celibacy in the adjoining room.

Kelly the Boy from Killane

He was a book of July flowers
from the middle of the county
that everyone wanted to open
at a particular page
to see that part of him.

Suddenly in memory Fintan
aging old flower of a solicitor
calls young waiters of
White's Hotel 'Ganymedes'.

I think 'The Balmoral Flirt'
they see a gold cigarette case.

Two or three days on
pedestrianised Main St.
I notice two or three
passable looking boys
I feel like Fintan O'Connor.

Cigarette in one hand
other hand in my hand
fresh air breathing
down from a Friary
moon on a summer night-
version of deep carouse
Mary Street knocked away
your hand your chest is
another moon on the
bell tower horizon
I touch the springs –
a summer night in which God
dies bodies too – knew love
love floated.

My sole delight is in Mary's pub
on John's Gate where the I.R.A. cubs
of N. Wexford 1940–1960 inlay their glories,
some my father's patients by Croghan's lorries.

STEVIE'S WILD ASHES

Knapsack, taking out of clean clothes. Cans of corn,
brown bread. The early worm,
Stevie had hiked the Christian cars on Sunday from Co.
Wexford.

Dark clothes like a clerical student in the shadows of
O'Connell Avenue. Limerick's bells
ring all the time.

In South's pub. Cousin John says, 'Look at the tapestries
in the back room'. Old Mr.
South pulling pints. Men of marriage before Sunday
dinner.

John, 'Are you in love with Stevie?' 'No, I just like him
    a lot'.

Now in The White House. Someone with his mother is
talking about the pub 'I tell you
what this is: it's a fairyhouse'. Mother, 'What's a
fairyhouse'. 'It's a place British Army
officers went to Easter Monday, 1916'.

I get Stevie to look at the gays, 'Look at the pretty one
with the cross'. John, 'You used
to have some compassion'.

Knows things, doesn't want them spilled out.

Stevie getting into bed. Black pyjama bottom. 'It's cold
... This is the first time I've done
this, would you like anything special'. 'I'm a Catholic,
all I want is an old fashioned
fuck'. 'I hope I didn't rush you'.

Underpants on the second night.

Stevie's valediction, 'When you're writing to me don't put your name on the outside.
The letters could be waiting all day on the table'.

ALL AROUND MY HAT I WEAR PEACE COLOURED RIBBONS O

I

Francis Stuart retires to Valhalla to his friends
I wear a yellow sweater
classroom youth are Cavafy-beautiful
shimmer in the skin of their poems

however every day opens dove light
I have to put my will into these orbits

My birthday cake that looks like Columba
Marmion 'A commandment I give you eat cake'

This moment of cake heyday light o memories

II

Fifty years ago Mervyn Doyne
said in the Woodenbridge Hotel
I was lowering birthday drinks
'I've been trying the Duke of Norfolk's remedy'
(gout) the hotelier Major Binstead had a German wife
the Plunketts (Lady Fitzwilliam's siblings)
had taken the estate workers down to the pub
Hester and David Plunkett and his girlfriend
Mary Williams the whiskey heiress
'jarred' started to order sandwiches

the German wife misheard 'sandbags'
she remembered the war too

28 years old I started to wear peace colours

III

Pax

Men if you don't know war pay for it
if we could only stick to peace 'foolishness'

(Teacher if you're a teacher pupil if a pupil
start peace lessons now

there's dancing and living in it)
please drink only with peace citizens

Any schoolgirl or schoolboy can find a bottle
let them be nice

ask your nearest wine and cheese princess
about the next party for peace mouths

but the hot officer corps didn't understand no win
didn't understand women and children pay

my 5th 6th 7th 8th 9th 10th birthdays
my parents drank them during World War II

while soldier-artists
read in sullen Paris cafes

IV

God

was born in a Concentration Camp
as the guards celebrated winter solstice

He was taken from his parents and
given illegally to a German family

the family was visited by three S.S. officers
who played with the baby

the family was reported to Berlin he was
spirited to an East Prussian safe house

1945 the boy ran away to a Tubingen
commune he ruled in absolute kindness

That is not box office

CHRISTMAS EVE
for Sheila Roberts

The wife putting a candle in the midst of a holly
wreath, and placing it in the dining room window, said,
'The windows of East Clare are lighted up tonight in
case the Holy Family has nowhere to stay'. Under the
starred tree opening presents we'll be late for Mass,
we're always the family late for Mass, but then the
Doctor was different, half an atheist maybe but not his
wife. Then we'd go to a party, at the local lawyer's, and
the Doctor, maybe for the first time in the year would
go on the batter, and there'd be ructions. He'd have
scoops of gin, be as moldy as Lord Iveagh. Would we
get safely home the three miles to the house, without
being put out on the side of the road and walking over
the snow? We arrived for the ham, turkey, spiced beef
from granny in Limerick, Heidsieck, brandy lighted on
the plum pudding brandy butter by it. We wore party
hats at the table and pulled crackers, now more than
one adult was langers, this time the American wife, and
one or both of them would soon exit slamming the
door. If we were unlucky this happened before the
King's Speech at three o'clock, George VI with his
stammer out of an old German Bible.

Christmas Eve 1950

Bobby was coming back from Woodenbridge Golf Club, he wanted to offer season's wishes to Clare. Bobby drove into the yard and knocked on the door, Josie in the kitchen was terrified, it was late. At last Josie opened the door, Bobby stopped himself from putting his arms around her. He went through the hall to the drawing room, a lady was sitting by the fire. 'This is a nice thing, to appear at this hour, I haven't seen you in a while'. 'Clare, you won't mind when you see what I have brought', he was hiding a bottle of Haig scotch – her favourite – behind his back ... A lady sitting by her fire drank a scotch and ginger ale. She was not the kind to put her arms around Bobby. He had got the whisky from Maisie Kelly in Wolohan's, an old Blue Shirt house, it was still scarce after the war. General Collins's photograph over the fireplace smiled.

Mother Goes Home

I

The first olive green trains of the
Dublin Area Rapid Transport noiselessly
glided through freshly painted stations
the same moment (Monday July 23)
that mother died ... she cries and
weeps for the lovely days
she is forgotten as though she is male.
Her body travels along the coast
on the curving sea-near line
in an olive coach perfumed by song.
See what escorts her that seem like clouds
Co. Clare farmers carrying sticks to the fair
immigrants with boat tickets
crumpled addresses in New York
evictees with small bags of clothes.
Three faces make her welcome
The Blessed Virgin the Statue of Liberty
and Kathleen Ni Houlihan
all in new clothes.

II

First there were Bohemians
who talked while they made love
Then career saints. Then the
holy barbarians who had a saint
called Kerouac ... they sang
crusader songs in the groin.
The people she saw
called out to each other
'How's the book going?'

Mother was on these streets
with her school bag
as she stepped out of the limousine
on her way to the
Convent of the Sacred Heart
Her soul is in the parlour
in Grant's tomb
spread out along Riverside Drive.
In the Village she heard
cabaret jazz musicians
early polyphony McCormack
from the tavern door.

    III

On her head a crown of shamrocks and laurels.

Tom Walsh, K.M.

Three doctors spelled out 'festival'
broke the Light Opera's singing spine.

The young intern reading scores Eva
player of the ivories caressed his neck
in the Old Pound House.

Opera the works
bowtied doctor at La Scala in season's heat
Glynbourne autumn garden of libettos.

The old house cygnet stopped twinkling
on a cruise ship he saw another cigarette
holder green jewel case.

Three doctors led by Compton MacKenzie
arrived from The Gramaphone Society
to a Cathedral of an opera house

in a narrow street
as the last Court of Europe dipped to a
bourgeois class divas entered Wexford

painted noblemen's faces raspberry tones of
Lady Gregory's nephew and Lord and
Lady Harewood in twilight combat.

I beheld a doctor of the three head honcho
a knight of anesthesia with clubmen
reliving The Bohemian Girl.

(To swim in Mallarme's 'mysterious festival'
an Inn of voices that shelter the structureless).

Departing 2 Lower George's Street
to board the ferry at Rosslare
in Knight of Malta uniform
on pilgrimage sword in scabbard

the English purser asks, 'Expecting trouble
Sir', the festival director like the singer
awakens with the naked sword.

Omos do Funge

There are sleepers and wakers, the sleepers are below
 ground
underground, they don't always have obscure names.
You know the wakers who know the sleepers,
sometimes wakers are open-eyed they see wankers.

Short working song:
Paris Review wanks
Dublin Review wanks,
that slightly higher order of celebratory narcissism
Art News keeps on wanking.

Shorter working song:
academy sleepers and wakers
specially tenured sleepers,
watch out even wakers when we dead awaken.

Networking is not quality time, whoring may be nice,
or actually meeting people having some witty desire in
 the night
moving through the fair with a flair touch of heart.
Alright or bless that.

Enda Keane, O.F.M.

Dawn of the state, the cheering and the bullets
then a renegade Corkman in The Lodge,
an American in the Under Secretary's Lodge,
a Friar Minor in the Chief Secretary's Lodge,
Fr. Enda a chaplain to it all secretary to a Friar
Pascal Robinson Representative of the Representative.
The Nuncio had the ears Enda the typing skills
the giving hand with the Curia's hospitality when
a distraught Anglo-Irishman needed steadying.
To be President to have your Roscommon poteen,
bowed drooping moustache revived by
each drop to rambling of a tweed-clad seanachai.
Government Buildings: not another swallow,
straight out the back door to the Nunciature
where legal whiskey shone an Assumption moon
on the petticoats of Connaught where the poets
endured on whiskey not porridge perhaps
something of the creature poured on the gruel.
Secular Excellency put to bed Pius XI not told.
To have revived a language and instead get a state
and a celestial shebeen in Phoenix Park.
Enda was present when the German Minister
knelt to kiss Pascal Robinson's ring
so Hitler wired instantaneous dismissal.
Assumptions later Enda lowered a bottle
with mother with ancient seminary giggles,
retold the stories (thousand and one shaky nights
of the Free State), repeated the stories
over and over mother rolled her eyes,
he presented my sister with the bullet fired
over Collins's grave gift of Joe O'Reilly
(my sister can't find it), happy at last
because Fr. Guardian allowed his pension
I pulled him against the Wexford Friary door

rang the bell and ran back to the car.
Son of Assisi, allow Enda a little vow-breaking
St. Clare understands he did not wish to abandon
poverty yet he deserved prizes on earth.
I poured stiff ones into the glass in his hand,
in the morning he lay in his robes between
two beds, I'll put a golden crown on his head.

May, Queen of Inch

They were all after May, bank clerks, creamery
      managers,
Aidan Mernagh was crazy about her.
They'd go on spins down to the beach. She had a red
      Citroen.
She had an album of her boyfriends, she'd laugh over it.

The Byrnes employed May in the Post Office, their sons
      got a car
and toured all Ireland. They gambled, male madness of
      summer.
Everyone went bankrupt in those days, their father
      wouldn't.
'I'll pay my debts, a pound for a pound. The children
      can go
to America and get a start'.

Across the road, the O'Brien-Hennessys bought the
      pub.
American accents. They brought their old grandmother
      from
New Ross, black coat and pipe. She used to sit in the
      evening
after ten in the window.

May went up three quarters of a mile to her Post Office
in Coolgreany. She did Children's allowances, Radio
      licenses,
savings accounts. She took out her stamp collection or
the minutes of the evicted tenants of the Brooks Estate
(up to 1932). She brought down the album of her old
      boyfriends
and laughed over it.

THAT HOUSE AGAIN

I sleep for the last night
swallows in the sheds
blue and yellow jockey photo
on the wall of the groom's house
horse stalls next door
steep stairs to the loft

Late yard summer night
bluesy Venus clear Plough
as we do our afterpub pissing
light shines in the house
a friend uses the bathroom

I am thinking of how many flowers
my mother grew
in the yard in the garden in herself
Roses of colour

The village fled from Wexford
it has forgotten grandmothers
I had waved to the parade
of passion and story
that has flayed the street.

How was the evacuation
for ever and then three weeks
selecting and boxing pre-auction
trestles for the viewing
the yard the front full of hands
after auction carrying to storage
what was not sold

Patients medical salesmen bridge players
Kavanagh stood by the door

Ashbery crawled by the rose beds
Hartnett hid in the attic

(Snaps)
what mother is (posh)
what father does
(fills medicine bottles)

A stillness not a taking
monkey puzzle tree for fun
copper beech for peace
Did you perish
The house was a womb with all its defects and yet

DEAD TENNIS COURT

I

In Yeats and Moore: balustrades,
swans, staircases, choruses of them,
specially on the wallpaper.
fairied in a double sense
he becomes part of the county
of compound ghosting.
Hope is like gold under the ground,
part of this wallpaper is heaven on earth.
He finds himself hiding behind a cloud
as if he was born from the dead.

II

I arrange a tryst 'a talk:'
under a palm tree of a dead
tennis court, if there are elves
please carry around our notebook.
the garden may be a cake with
a white beach in the middle of it.
he maiden me death he death me maiden.
Schubert's Tennis Masque,
more of the sound over the eternal July
of your net. We lie wrapped
in the games of summer.

III

Passion is about the life
and death of all us maidens.
Desire is a composition by awe,
a clock's trembling strings
clock with random hands.

Though they do not say this
in village bars about boys
we must be alert to the beautiful:
hair dyed blonder, neck
and shoulder in black T-shirt,
eyelids galante. I put the beautiful
here under the protection of evanescence.

   IV

Me from the University of Wisconsin
him a moonshiner from Tennessee,
take our places in summer.

I Sing of the English

The train drew into the dark of Woodenbridge
they had spent the hot day in the city with small flags,
Edwardus Septimus had passed with the horse-plums,
he had seen them and waved, she was four years old
her mother had spent time dressing her up for the day.
They made their way with the stars on Bayley's woods
over the bridge that once must have been made of
    wood
to a yeoman's house at the start of the Slate Quarry
    road.

A landlord with the biggest house in England the
    grandest
woods in Ireland he sauntered over in the summer to
view his house and trees, he sailed into Arklow harbour
his yacht followed by that of Sir Thomas Lipton
they went up on the railway from Woodenbridge
which the landlord suggested the Government build.
He exercised le droit, his tenants sent teenage daughters
up to the Big House for abatement of the rent.

The landlord loved his agent who doubled as an
intelligence agent for the Castle, he traveled from
the Shillelagh station via Woodenbridge to make his
    reports,
on the platform at Westland Row Collins's crew got
    him.
The day Collins was shot Lord Fitzwilliam was not at
Coolatin but rolled from the Sherlbourne Hotel to the
Kildare Street Club treating acquaintances, 'It cost me
dear but I had to have that man fixed, to level things'.

The little girl grew up she returned to the city, she was
    in

a Cafe off Aungier Street snipers shot out the glass
on the frames of Queen Mary and King George,
she heard the bands playing up and down the quays
Dublin was beside itself with Jacks and cheers:
the boys and girls were coming home from the front.
At Westland Row she kissed an aunt who carried her
present down railway carriage steps, a stuffed French
    bear.

In Limerick in a house called Avondale my mother was
    puzzled
by cheering she heard from O'Connell Street as far out
    as
Corbally, her brother arrived home with a Roches
    Stores
shopping bag emblazoned with a Jack, he had to take it
    back.
My father saw a Welsh Fusilier kicked on Catherine
    Street
by a crowd, rescued by people who put him in their
    house.
The day Churchill was buried St. Saviour's bells in
Arklow rang from breakfast on over the Irish town.

FIRE PHOENIX PYRE

Glossy photos that revealed the doctors who are knights of Columbanus, the singers supported by the knights, Richard King's mildly 1890s Celtic church paintings purchased by the knights, the bog cotton of the 1950s.

The heavy *Capuchin Annual* you'd think you'd need a forklift to hold it up.

The singer who was the printer said, 'The editor's brown robes with cord in the Gresham Lounge: Fr. Senan stood out in contrast to Peadar O'Donnell a suburban lapsed Catholic. Their table piled high with cakes. Their magazines seemed to eat them. I had a few of the cakes myself so I ended up printing the Annual which included driving Fr. Senan around. He'd want to go here, he'd want to go there, he'd come down to Wexford to look at the proofs, that would take several days, I looked after him. I drove him back to Dublin once with my aunt English, we had to stop at the Montrose for a meal, I never saw a man for the eating like that. Then he wanted to go to the Phoenix Park, I said I had to go back to Wexford. I left him somewhere on Sandymount Road in what looked like a derelict house, it was in the dark the windows broken. Maybe he wanted me to feel bad. Did you knew he was expelled from the Order when the whole thing blew up? He was sent to Australia like Fr. Albert and the other Capuchins who brought the host to the condemned men of 1916. Father Gerard came round and asked how much is owed for printing most of the back issues, it was paid weekly after that, I tell you never work for the Catholic Church, there will always be a discount. He was one of the Magi alright'.

Life of the Fianna

I was a young lad in Carlow in the thirties up to my eyes in the IRA. The great organiser in the area was a man called Peadar McGuinness. He was educated, he had books in his cottage and a gramophone with records. He was a great big man who loved to talk – the poor fellow died on hunger strike afterwards. One night when we were walking back from Carlow, it was a fine warm night with a young moon.
As we came to the place where the lanes to our places forked off we stopped. All of a sudden he came over and put his arms around me and kissed me. I got a terrible shock and cried out, 'If you ever do that again I'll kill you'.

He stepped back from me and started to weep.

He said, 'If I'm like that it was Padraic Pearse who made me'.

JACOBINS

Sitting in McDaid's with Katherine Kavanagh, I wear the badge of the Jacobites, the Fine Gael party. A group further down starts shouting 'Labour'. 'Why are you wearing that? Mrs. Kavanagh, I'm surprised at you sitting beside him'. Katherine to me, 'Have you a second one? Give it to me'. 'Mrs. Kavanagh, I'm surprised at you. Your husband ... He owes his seat on the Canal to Labour'. Katherine, 'I have it on because you attacked my friend. Paddy was not like that, he was never for Labour. He was Fine Gael first and last ...' Chorus of shouts, 'Labour, Labour, get them. Ashamed they should be!'

Evensong in Wexford Town

In the Chancery: Brendan poetic and unruly says
'Make the most liberal interpretation'.

Bishop Caulfields's anathema sits on Vinegar Hill
but it's for sale, tanning salons?

St. Adjutor up the lane patron of
those underage and dry

(people far from towns had a saying about priests
follow their teaching but don't bother with their ways
fairies were the housekeepers who had everything
    clean
and clear-cut, the fairies and the priests ran the dances
Christ's new wounds aren't the wounds of the people
they're the new vinegar the priests must drink).

The priest at Tagoat says Musgrave's History
of the Rebellion is correct.

Truth is the Romancer of history
he is also the auctioneer who will have the Friary listed
for sale, will my sister buy it?

Brendan lovely sybarite bishop on the plane to
    America.

AT YOUR HOLY MOUTH

After a hymn they
went to the Mount of Olives.
Else Lasker-Schuler rose from
the dead before them wearing
her rags and belt. She spoke,
'I have been like the master,
I lived on handouts for years,
I am hidden in the inns,
I break bread to give crumbs
to birds, I order a glass of wine
to observe people and salvation,
are you ready for a new hymn,
can we join in singing it together?'

About the Author

James Liddy was born in Lr. Pembroke St., Dublin, in 1934. His parents hailed from the cities of Limerick and New York. He lived in Coolgreany, County Wexford, intermittently from 1941 to 2000. His many books include *Blue Mountain* (Dolmen, 1968), *A Munster Song of Love and War* (White Rabbit, 1971), *Baudelaire's Bar Flowers* (Capra/White Rabbit, 1975), *Corca Bascinn* (Dolmen, 1977), *Collected Poems* (Creighton University, 1994), *Gold Set Dancing* (Salmon, 2000), *I Only Know that I Love Strength in My Friends and Greatness* (Arlen House, 2003), *On the Raft with Fr. Roseliep* (Arlen House, 2006) and *The Askeaton Sequence* (Arlen House, 2009). With Paul Vogel he has published two books of Mandelstam versions, *Sophias* and *Death Row*.

He is a professor in the English Department at the University of Wisconsin-Milwaukee where he teaches creative writing and Irish and Beat literature. *James Liddy: A Critical Study* by Brian Arkins was published by Arlen House in 2001 and the widely acclaimed *Honeysuckle, Honeyjuice: A Tribute to James Liddy* edited by Michael Begnal appeared in 2006.

The first volume of his memoir, *The Doctor's House: An Autobiography* was published by Salmon in 2004, with volume two, *The Full Shilling,* forthcoming from Salmon.